C000252491

AROUND
BLANDFORD
FORUM
IN OLD PHOTOGRAPHS

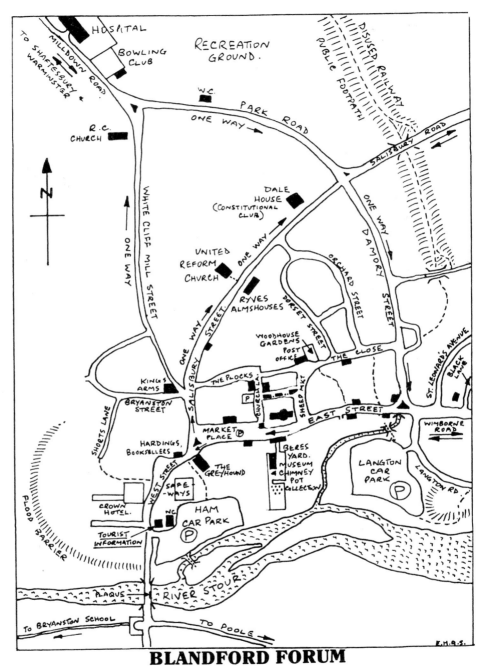

BLANDFORD FORUM

(Map by Eric Schmidt)

AROUND
BLANDFORD FORUM
IN OLD PHOTOGRAPHS

COLLECTED BY
BEN COX

ALAN SUTTON
1989

Alan Sutton Publishing Limited
Brunswick Road · Gloucester

First published 1989

Copyright © 1989 Benjamin G. Cox

All rights reserved. No part of this publication may be reproduced, stored in a retrieval system, or transmitted, in any form or by any means, electronic, mechanical, photocopying, recording or otherwise, without the prior permission of the publishers and copyright holders

British Library Cataloguing in Publication Data

Around Blandford Forum in old photographs.
1. Dorset. Blandford Forum, history
I. Cox, Ben
942.3'32

ISBN 0-86299-618-X

Cover picture: Blandford Forum Market Place decorated for 1897 Jubilee celebrations.

Typesetting and origination by
Alan Sutton Publishing Limited.
Printed in Great Britain
by Dotesios Printers Limited.

CONTENTS

INTRODUCTION 6

1. BLANDFORD FORUM – THE MARKET TOWN 9

2. PEOPLE 49

3. OUR NEAR NEIGHBOURS 89

4. THE MILITARY 143

ACKNOWLEDGEMENTS 160

And there came Stoure with terrible aspect,
Baring his six deformed heads on hye;
That doth his course through Blandford plains direct,
and washeth Wimborne meades in seasons drye.

from Edmund Spenser's (1590–96) *The Faerie Queene.*

Blandford is a flourishing borough and market town containing 500 houses, many of them built of stone. It is a thoroughfare on the coach road to Exeter. No town hereabouts has so great a number of gentlemens seats round about it as this, invited hither perhaps by the pleasant downs adjoining which can hardly be equalled in the world. It is now one of the most considerable towns of the county for travellers.

Daniel Defoe 1724

BLANDFORD FORUM MARKET PLACE C. 1900 with brewery dray outside The Red Lion Inn and hay waggon outside the town hall.

INTRODUCTION

This selection of old photographs is intended to provide a nostalgic peep into the past of the old market town of Blandford Forum, of the villages around it, of the military camp which for many years has been accepted as an important and valued part of our local community and of the people who lived in these places, their vocations and some of their leisure activities recorded on glass plates or film and going back to when photography started in mid Victorian times. The district was not well blessed with skilled photographers in the early period but such professionals as we had in Blandford itself were very good. What a shame it is that so many of the photographs one sees bear no record of the place, date or persons photographed, thus precluding most of them from inclusion in this collection. We can all learn from this I am sure!

Blandford Forum itself has been a market town and borough since the early Middle Ages. Its prosperity grew by virtue of the fact that it was on an important river crossing and that it was ideally situated to provide services required in connection with the extensive sheep farming on the downs surrounding the town and from agriculture generally. It became famous for its markets and sheep fairs, its grammar school, breweries, coaching inns and all the professional services, craftsmen and tradespeople needed to serve the area with which we are concerned. It was on the main London to Exeter coaching route and the hotel industry provided considerable local employment. The town grew and grew and had to expand into the adjoining parishes of Pimperne, Bryanston and Langton Long.

As the town centre of Blandford Forum is a strictly controlled conservation area, famous for its Georgian houses, church, market place and town hall, there has been little change in its general appearance since it was rebuilt after the great fire of 1731 which destroyed over 90 per cent of the town. This being so, it has been difficult to date some town-centre photographs — one usually has to go by the clothing worn or by the vehicles appearing in the pictures. I've learned a lot about dating old motor cars!

Nearly all the villages around Blandford have the River Stour or its tributaries, the Tarrant and the East Winterbourne, passing through them — the others are on the downlands overlooking the river valleys. A large proportion of the land in these nearby villages originally formed part of the Bryanston estates of the Portman family. The family acquired much of the land in the mid seventeenth century from the original lords of the manor, the Rogers family, who had been in possession as tenants-in-chief since 1399 but who ran out of male heirs in the 1600s. With additional purchases the Portman family built their estates up to a holding of over 7000 acres spread over parts of Blandford Forum, Bryanston, Durweston, Knighton, Stourpaine, Hamoon, Shillingstone and elsewhere. Nearly everybody in those places was a tenant and/or employee of the Portmans who provided most of the amenities enjoyed by their tenantry. The beginning of the end of this neo-feudal community, which had lasted some 800 years, came in 1925 when the principal manor house at Bryanston, which the family were no longer living in, was sold off to become the Bryanston Public School as it is today. Most of the remainder was taken over by the Crown in 1950 in satisfaction of heavy claims for estate duties arising from the deaths of the second to the seventh Viscounts Portman between 1919 and 1948. Most of the other villages in the area had, since early medieval times, been the property of the great Abbeys of Milton, Shaftesbury and Tarrant Crawford which were sold off after the Dissolution of the Monasteries in the 1530s to a new class of wealthy merchants, diplomats, members of parliament and others wishing to become country landowners in this favoured area. These were the builders of our large country houses, farms and cottage properties. The people working on these great estates provided the goods on which Blandford Forum depended for its markets and fairs and prosperity generally. The Squire, the Parson and the Schoolmaster ran these village estate communities to the satisfaction of most. The workers' dwellings were provided by the landlords. After the Second World War there was a gradual exodus of farm and domestic workers. Their cottages have now been beautifully restored and embellished though now mostly occupied as holiday or retirement homes.

The third group of families making up the Blandford and district community, although constantly changing, are the troops and their families and the civilian workers living or working at Blandford Camp on the downs in Pimperne and Tarrant Monkton parishes and roughly on the site of the former Blandford Racecourse. There have been soldiers quartered there, on and off, since long before the Napoleonic wars. They mostly came for training in times when there was a danger of invasion, when troops were needed for sending overseas, and at times when some sort of uprising or civil commotion was feared.

Early in the present century these downs were used for military reviews, summer camps and training grounds by the Dorset Rifle Volunteers, the Dorset Imperial Yeomanry and troops from other counties who found the terrain ideal for the purpose. In the First World War a hutted camp was erected to accommodate the Royal Naval Division and other units. It was to this RND Camp that the famous war poet, Rupert Brooke, came in 1914 and where he penned, on Blandford Camp notepaper, his best known poem 'The Soldier' which began:

If I should die think only this of me
That there's some corner of a foreign field
That is for ever England . . .

A lot of literary types got sent down to Blandford at this time and his friends included Arthur Asquith, son of the then Prime Minister, A.P. Herbert, Vere Harmsworth, son of Lord Rothermere, and Bernard Freyberg a New Zealander who later won the VC and three DSOs. In the Second World War he commanded, as a Lieut. General, the 2nd New Zealand Division in Italy. Sadly, Rupert Brooke died in 1915 aboard ship on his way to see service abroad and was buried on the island of Skyros.

Towards the end of the First World War, Blandford Camp became a training centre for recruits to the newly formed Royal Air Force and the site of the RAF Records Office. Soon after the war all units at the camp were dispersed and the huts sold off to farmers and others leaving the land to revert to grazing.

In 1939 Blandford Camp was back in use for military purposes and tented accommodation was provided for the first military conscripts to be called up that summer under the Act of that year establishing conscription. Huts were again built and occupied by various troops sent there from various corps for battle training. In 1943/4 a large part of the camp was taken over and adapted by the United States Army for its 22nd General Hospital to receive and give treatment to combat forces who became casualties in the European theatre of war. In due course it became very busy, particularly during the 'Battle of the Bulge', when some 500 casualties would be flown in from France in a single day to the nearby Tarrant Rushton airfield to be conveyed to the Camp hospital within hours of becoming casualties

Nearly all the old wooden huts used by the Americans have now gone and we have a very extensive range of modern buildings, administration blocks, theatre, cinema, married quarters and the magnificent museum of the Royal Corps of Signals, the present occupiers of the Camp, who have their School of Signals there. Blandford Camp is like a little town of its own but, being so close to Blandford Forum, it has become very important to Blandford's economy and provides work for many civilians residing in the town and district. The famous Royal Corps of Signals military band is also stationed at the Camp and they frequently perform in the town for the benefit of local charities. Altogether the town and camp enjoy a very happy relationship.

The Market Town

BLANDFORD FORUM MARKET PLACE c. 1920. On the left can be seen part of the printing office of William Shipp who was co-editor of the third edition of *Hutchins History of Dorset* 1873. It is now W.H. Smiths.

PHILLIP ABRAHAM BARNES, Alderman and one of the last of the Blandford wool-staplers. He was Mayor of the borough seven times. His brother, John Iles Barnes, was Mayor eight times. They were great benefactors to the town and provided, among other things, the Barnes Homes and the swimming baths.

THE MAYOR, ALBERT H. HILLYER, reads the Proclamation of King Edward VII – January 1901 – outside the town hall.

THE OPENING OF THE BARNES HOMES in Salisbury Road in 1909. They were built by John Iles Barnes in memory of his brother, Phillip Abraham Barnes. The land was purchased from the Portman Estate.

THOMAS NESBITT (1850–1923?), last of the Nesbitt family of Blandford photographers who started in this business in 1864. He was a town councillor and Borough Auditor.

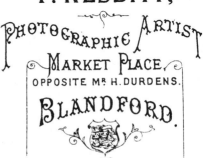

THOMAS NESBITT'S TRADE CARD indicating royal patronage. He was often called to local country houses to take photographs when members of the royal family were visiting.

PREMISES OF EDGAR B. SMITH & SON, Tailors of 26/28 Market Place, Blandford. Edgar B. Smith was an Alderman of the Borough and Mayor 1884/85. The premises are now those of Howard Hall, Estate Agents.

BLANDFORD MARKET PLACE taken from the west in the 1920s showing the front of the former Greyhound Hotel on the right. It was the National Provincial Bank at the time of the photograph.

A BIRD'S EYE VIEW OF THE TOWN taken around 1906 from the roof of the Blandford St Mary
Brewery of Hall & Woodhouse Ltd.

THE JUNCTION OF SALISBURY STREET WITH WHITE CLIFF MILL STREET c. 1885, showing offices of the former Blandford Express Newspaper and snow clearing activities.

SALISBURY STREET, Blandford, in the 1890s taken from outside Tom Nesbitt's studio. The shop on the right, Durdens, is probably the oldest in Blandford having been established in 1713 and still in business today.

SALISBURY STREET. Another view with the street decorated for King Edward VII's Coronation. Tom Nesbitt's studio is on the left.

SALISBURY STREET in 1890 following a severe blizzard.

SALISBURY STREET looking down towards the Market Place c. 1905. George Dyke's watchmaking business can be seen on left. This area was demolished to make way for Woolworths.

BLANDFORD'S SHOE SHOP established in 1873. This picture at 29 Salisbury Street is of a date c. 1920. Outside are Miss E.F. Blandford and Mr H. Blandford.

INTERNATIONAL STORES in Salisbury Street, c. 1930. From left to right: Graham White, Joe Blandford, Mr Fry, Mr Stroud, Fred Gould.

THOMAS NESBITT'S STUDIO — originally part of the old Bell Inn property in Salisbury Street.

CHARLES CRAMP, in the doorway of his butcher's shop in Salisbury Street around 1920. It is now Senior & Godwin (Prudential) Estate Agency.

THE GEORGE INN at 26 Salisbury Street (formerly known as The Three Swans) was one of the town's oldest pubs, having been licensed from 1791 until 1965.

THE WESTCOTT FAMILY took over this watchmaking and jewellery business at 5 Market Place from William Wyatt in around 1890. Edwin Westcott and his children are in the right-hand doorway and his shop assistant and errand boy are in the left-hand one. This picture was taken around 1908.

THIS ATTRACTIVE SHOP at 6 Salisbury Street was for many years the watch and clock business of Eyers & Kerridge. It is a survivor of many old bow-fronted shops built soon after the fire of 1731.

E.D. HORSEY had a prosperous business here in 1906 next to the Congregational Chapel (now United Reformed) in Salisbury Street. The premises still have his iron display gantry and it is still a butcher's shop.

WHITE CLIFF MILL STREET, looking down towards the corner of Salisbury and Bryanston Street. Fianders Garage is on the right near the front and Dowdings the saddlers is in the distance with the Temperance Hotel on the left, c. 1920.

THE PEOPLES FURNITURE STORES in Upper Salisbury Street was established by J.W. Blandford in 1889. It is still a furniture shop but is now owned by John Dixon.

THE OLD FIRE STATION at North Place, Blandford. It has since been demolished to be replaced by residential accommodation.

PARK ROAD in around 1910. The Archbishop Wake School and the Cottage Hospital can be seen in the far distance.

PARK PLACE, Blandford, in around 1912 – one of the most exclusive parts of the town in those days.

THE FORMER COUNTY POLICE STATION in Salisbury Road was erected in 1859 following the formation of a county force. The property is now called d'Arcy Court.

THE UNION WORKHOUSE in Salisbury Road was built in 1858 to replace former cramped accommodation in East Street. Most of the workhouse was demolished in 1970. What is left is known as Castleman Homes. In its day this was deemed by tramps to have the best casual ward in the county.

WAREHAM & ARSCOTT'S GROCERY at 23 Salisbury Street. The property was known as Harewood House so, originally, it probably belonged to the Portman family, the first Viscount having married a daughter of the Earl of Harewood.

INSIDE MARKWELLS, another firm of grocers, who had premises in the Market Place where the National Westminster Bank is now. It belonged to the George family for many years.

A GROUP standing outside the old Post Office in West Street c. 1906. Another group can be seen inspecting the floods outside the Crown Hotel.

WEST STREET looking towards the Market Place, 1910. Conyers Garage is in the distance. The blinds on the front left of the picture are shading Bishop's shoe shop.

J.J. HICKS original outfitters shop at 7 West Street c. 1875. The business flourished and became a large department store under Alex J. Hicks with branches at Wareham and Sturminster Newton.

PART OF THE HICKS DEPARTMENT STORE in West Street in the 1930s.

BLANDFORD MOTOR WORKS in West Street. This property was formerly part of the town's Assembly Rooms. This photograph is of 1907 and there is still a garage business there.

ROBERT SHARP AND HIS DAUGHTER outside their garden shop at 23 West Street. Mr Sharp was a regular prize winner at local shows and had other premises at Blandford St Mary.

THE CROWN, Blandford's principal hotel, c. 1910, showing a mixture of horse-drawn carriages and horseless ones.

MR A. LAMBERT, the Crown Hotel coachman c. 1905. He met the trains and transported guests as required.

GEORGE LOADER'S CYCLE SHOP when in Oakfield Street in around 1912. He later moved his business to East Street.

ERNEST G. FOOT'S DRAPERY was in West Street next to Conyers Gun Shop. This picture was taken c. 1928.

UPPER SALISBURY STREET (in some old deeds it is referred to as 'ye high streete'). The Ryves Almshouses are on the right and Mr Forsey the butcher is outside his shop opposite, c. 1914.

STAFF AND DELIVERY VANS outside Jeffery's bakery in Alexandra Street. They had been in business there at least as early as 1907.

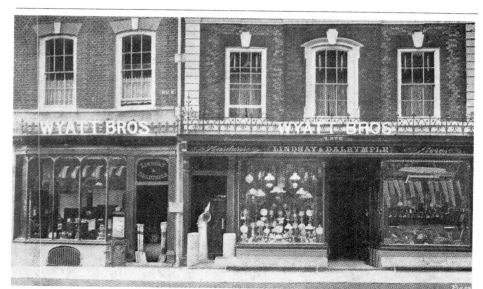

WYATT BROS. PREMISES in the Market Place showing the name of their predecessors, Lindsay & Dalrymple. This old established firm is still in business.

WORKERS EMPLOYED BY WYATT BROS. at their Market Place premises c. 1920. Left to right: Bert Conduit, Bill Wells (standing) ? Butt (with basket) and Jack New.

GEORGE SMART & SON were coal merchants, furniture removers and hauliers. They had their own railway trucks. Their premises were in Oakfield Street in 1906.

SALISBURY ROAD around 1914. Note the YMCA on the left and the large Fair Field with the Union Workhouse above it.

THE FORMER TOWN BREWERY of J.L. Marsh in Bryanston Street. The premises were demolished in 1987/8.

BLANDFORD DIRECTORY—1907.

Moderate Use of Stimulants !

Physical Improvement ! !

Eminent Doctors' Opinions :

Sir James Paget, Bart., F.R.C.S.,D.C.L.,LL.D.,F.R.S.
"As for the opinion of the Medical Profession, they are, by a vast majority in favour of a moderate habitual use of alcoholic drinks, and there are sufficient reasons for believing that such an habitual use is on the whole generally beneficial."

Sir William Gull, Bart., M.D., F.R.C.P.,D.C.L.,F.R.S
" For men working hard, beer is a good form of food, to be recommended as a light feeding material."

T. Lauder Brunton, M.D., F.R.C.P., F.R.S.
"Alcohol is a true food."

Albert J. Bernays, Ph.D.
"A glass of Beer, when the day's work is done, can do no possible harm

R. Brudenell Carter, F.R.C.S
" I do not hesitate to say that the advocates of total abstinence are mistaken. I affirm, alike from my own experience and from that of others, that there are some to whom it is a necessity if they are to exert the full measure of their power."

Alfred B. Garrod, M.D., F.R.C.P., F.R.S.
" The majority of adults can take a moderate quantity of alcohol not only with impunity, but often with advantage."

Sir Dyce Duckworth, M.D., LL.D., F.R.C.P.
Hon. Ph. to H.R.H the Prince of Wales, now His Majesty the King
" I believe the use of alcohol to be beneficial to humanity. In strict moderation I see nothing harmful, but on the contrary much that is beneficial in the present stage of our civilisation."

The late Rt. Hon. W. E. Gladstone said :
" Bitter Beer was a divine drink."

Tea taken in excess has been proved to be more harmful than Malt and Hop Beers in moderation.

Many very aged Persons in this Town and Neighbourhood are living instances of the beneficial effects of Moderate use of Stimulants.

Drink

MARSH'S Pure Malt and Hop ALES
And Live for ever.

The Brewery, Blandford.

ONE OF J.L. MARSH'S FAVOURITE ADVERTISEMENTS. If he drank his own beer he should still be alive!

THE ORIGINAL WESLEYAN CHAPEL in The Close built in 1834. Subsequently it was greatly enlarged and is still a place of worship.

BLANDFORD COTTAGE HOSPITAL founded by the Hon. L.E. Portman and Viscountess Portman in 1888 at Picket Close. The premises have recently been incorporated into Blandford's new Community Hospital.

THE OLD HOUSE in The Close is a survivor of the great fire of 1731. It was built in around 1650 by Frederick Sagitary, a Calvinist Protestant refugee from Germany. He had been Treasurer to His Highness the Palsgrave Elector Palatine of The Rhine.

THE PARISH CHURCH OF SS PETER AND PAUL at Blandford, taken from the east and showing the sign of the Star Inn on the left. There is no footpath below the church wall and the church railings.

WEST STREET taken from outside. The Crown. E.R. Ball's fish shop can be seen on the left.

BOATING ON THE STOUR at Blandford. This was quite popular until after the First World War. What a pity it is not revived.

A GENERAL VIEW TOWARDS BLANDFORD BRIDGE with the weir in the foreground.

FLOODS IN WEST STREET in 1892. Note Crown Hotel as it was prior to rebuilding and the town's assembly rooms on the right with a fine bay window overlooking the street.

DORSET

ANY PERSON WILFULLY INJURING ANY PART OF THIS COUNTY BRIDGE WILL BE GUILTY OF FELONY AND UPON CONVICTION LIABLE TO BE TRANSPORTED FOR LIFE BY THE COURT

7&8 GEO 4 C30 S13   T FOOKS

THE PENAL NOTICE of 1828 which is still on Blandford Bridge. It suggests an easy way of getting a trip to the Antipodes at public expense!

THIS BARN IN THE GREYHOUND YARD was built soon after the 1731 fire by the Bastard family who owned this famous coaching inn. It is still intact but the greater part of it is now used as professional offices. The barn was demolished to make space for the new Safeways.

THE FORMER MARKET TOLL HOUSE in the Greyhound Yard recently demolished to make way for Safeways. It could have been saved.

FIELDS OAK off Upper Salisbury Street is another magnificent property which had to be demolished to make way for a modern housing development.

EAST STREET looking west in around 1900. The corner premises were part of the old Union Workhouse, they were used as shops for many years but are now used as solicitors' offices.

EAST STREET c. 1905. Lyston House is on the right, with Munster House to the west of it, the latter providing an entrance to Tabernacle Walk shopping arcade.

STREET WORKS taking place in East Street in the late 1920s on the provision of the town's mains sewerage system.

THE BLUE BOAR INN at 10 East Street was there from 1865 to 1970. An earlier Blue Boar had been behind the town hall where the Corn Exchange is now. The East Street premises are now Thomas Hardy House.

THE PARISH CHURCH OF SS PETER AND PAUL was rebuilt between 1731 and 1739 after the great Blandford Fire. This photograph was taken in around 1910.

THE INTERIOR OF THE CHURCH prior to its being extended to the east in 1895 to provide a new chancel. Note the galleries erected in 1837. These were removed in 1971.

BLANDFORD STATION around 1880 with a shunting horse about to be employed. This was on the Somerset & Dorset Joint Railway which opened for passenger and goods traffic on 31 August 1863. It was closed for passengers on 7 March 1966 and for goods on 12 February 1967.

BLANDFORD STATION C. 1925 and much as it looked at the time it was closed.

ENGINE 41243 arriving at Blandford Station 18 June 1963 with passengers from Temple-combe to Bournemouth West. Photograph by Douglas E. Capewell, ARICS.

ENGINE 34107 *Blandford Forum*. One of the name plates can be seen in Blandford Town Hall Shambles.

BLANDFORD STATION shortly before the tracks were taken up c. 1970.

BLANDFORD RAILWAY BRIDGE was blown up on 25 July 1978. Lots were drawn for the honour of pressing the button. The price of petrol at the garage is interesting!

BLANDFORD MARKET PLACE decorated for the 1905/6 Tercentenary celebrations in respect of the granting of the Borough's Charter of Incorporation in 1605.

A DONKEY CART in East Street (?) c. 1885. It was used for bread deliveries but the surname is obscured by the wheel.

SECTION TWO

People

BLANDFORD TOWN COUNCIL at the time of Queen Victoria's Diamond Jubilee in 1897. Alderman E.B. Smith was Mayor. J.L. Marsh, whose brewery is shown in this collection, sits on the far right of the front row.

BLANDFORD CORPORATION in 1920. Louis B. Bunce, Boot & Shoe maker, was Mayor and his daughter sitting next to him was Mayoress.

MAYOR EDWARD DERHAM in the mayoral chair with mace-bearers F. Goddard and T. Barlett standing on either side. 1912.

BLANDFORD BOROUGH COUNCIL in 1912. Back row, left to right: Capt Walter, Cllr. Riggs, Cllr. Bunce, Cllr. Foot, Cllr. Webb, Supt. Sims, Cllr. Gould, Cllr. Best, Cllr. Hobbs, Cllr. Payne, the Surveyor. Front row, left to right: Cllr. Norman, Cllr. Woodhouse, The Rector, Ald. Smith, Cllr. Derham (Mayor) Ald. Ball, Ald. Curtis, Town Clerk, Cllr. Dyke.

BLANDFORD MARKET PLACE lit up at night in connection with the 1905/6 Charter Celebrations. As the town had no electricity at the time each of the thousands of candle-lit fairy lights in glass bowls had to be ignited more or less simultaneously.

REVD CHARLES HENRY FYNES-CLINTON, MA Rector of Blandford from 1877 to 1913. A century ago this year he founded the Blandford Church Guild. He was largely responsible for getting the church extended some 30 feet to the east so that a new chancel could be provided. The work was completed in 1895.

ALBERT BUTT, a member of Blandford Town Band for some years before the First World War.

BLANDFORD FORUM BRASS BAND who became National Champions in open competition at the Crystal Palace in 1863. Back row: T. Hunt, C. Eyers, J. Purton, R. Eyers (Bandmaster), W. Skivington, F. Hunt and G. Hewlett. Front row: E. Blanchard, H. Monkton, J. Skivington, R. Nicholls, I. Hunt and J. Baker. The drummer boy on the left was not identified.

THE TOWN BAND c. 1880 outside the then new County Police Station (d'Arcy House) in Salisbury Road.

THE TOWN BAND in 1905 in their flat caps, adopted in place of the former pill-box hats.

NEW'S BAND of 1910 – the inscription reads 'J. New's band – 4 Old Pals'. They look a somewhat unusual combination.

BLANDFORD'S FAMOUS MOUTH-ORGAN BAND c. 1905. Jack New – one of the '4 Old Pals' in the previous photograph – sits in the front with his dog. J.B. Wellen's Alfred Street premises are in the background.

BLANDFORD CYCLING CLUB outside the Cottage Hospital c. 1905. A lot of Blandford sportsmen were photographed here – probably because the hospital adjoined the recreation ground.

THE FIRST PALACE CINEMA, taken in 1925. It was closed when a new Palace Cinema was opened on the other side of the road. It was re-opened during the Second World War to cope with the many troops in the area seeking entertainment and the name changed to The Ritz. It was closed again after the war.

THE SECOND PALACE CINEMA opened in 1929. A more modern frontage was later built – the property is now part of the Gateway supermarket.

BLANDFORD RANGERS FOOTBALL CLUB 1908/9. One of the many teams in the town at this time.

BLANDFORD UNITED FC 1931/32. Front row: C. Penny, E.G. Wright, B.F. Hunt,? Neale (Capt.), G.M. Cutler, L.C. Haim, L.G. Goringe. Middle row: R. Light (Hon.Sec.) O.J. Morris, A.C. Newman (Vice Capt.), T.R. Barnett, W.G. Cookman, E.R. Bellows, M.S. Joyce, B.C. Hunt (Chairman). Back row: W. Cookman, L.C. Preston, A.H. Blandford (Hon. Treas.), A.W. Cornick (Team Manager), C.W. Witt, G. Cox, E.C. Stickley.

BLANDFORD CRICKET CLUB 1924. *The Salisbury & Winchester Journal* of 2 June 1834 reported the Club as meeting 'on the new ground'.

THE FOOTLIGHT FOLLIES. This was a very popular local concert party in the 1960s — their shows were given in the Palace Cinema.

CAPT. WALTERS, Officer in Charge of the Blandford Volunteer Fire Brigade for many years between the wars.

BLANDFORD VOLUNTEER FIRE BRIGADE c. 1900 with their horse-drawn engine in Greyhound Yard. Opinions vary as to how long it took to catch and harness the horses!

BLANDFORD OPERATIC SOCIETY'S PRODUCTION of *The Mikado* in 1928.

THE OPERATIC SOCIETY'S PRODUCTION in 1927 was *Iolanthe*.

ONE OF THE FIRST CARS TO BE SEEN IN BLANDFORD was this Humberette two-seater of 1903. The registration letters *BF* were at first thought suitable for Blandford Forum but the drivers objected to being called the *BF*s. Mr G.W. Holdway of Child Okeford wrote this about the first car he saw in Blandford:

'I saw the first motor car. It belonged to a circus family visiting the town and created a great deal of excitement. It had solid rubber tyres about half an inch in diameter. It was driven through the streets at about four miles per hour. A man briskly waving a red flag trotted about 100 yards ahead. About 100 cheering children ran behind. The car made a noise like a threshing machine. The horses both old and young bolted up side streets and would not face this new invention which has since displaced them'.

A DE DION BOUTON of early pattern parked in Shorts Lane, Blandford, c. 1902.

THE LADIES OF BLANDFORD WESLEYAN CHAPEL leave town for a charabanc outing, c. 1920.

THE GREYHOUND INN OUTING CLUB ready to leave for a day trip on August Monday 1924 to Bridport and Lyme Regis. Looks like it was a wet day!

A STEAM ROLLER of Fredk. Sharp & Sons of Blandford called 'The Pride of Dorset'. The Sharp family had premises in Oakfield Street and at St Leonards Farm in 1906.

POST OFFICE STAFF at the old Post Office premises in West Street in 1934, shortly before the office was moved to new premises at The Tabernacle.

INTERIOR OF THE OLD POST OFFICE in West Street — from all the advertising matter it would seem there was a sales drive on to get people to become telephone subscribers.

OPENING OF THE NEW BLANDFORD HEAD POST OFFICE at The Tabernacle by Alderman Miss E.G. Castleman-Smith in 1935. She was Blandford's first lady Mayor.

STAFF AND VEHICLES outside the new Post Office at Blandford c. 1938. In those days the main entrance to the counter was to the left of the main building.

MR TOM COUSINS, for 40 years a postman at Blandford. The stripes on his left breast indicate his years of service.

MRS JAY, wife of William Jay of East Street, Blandford. She was one of Blandford's Second World War postwomen.

POST OFFICE STAFF outside the new Post Office, c. 1935. Left to right: Mr T. Haines, Mr H. Elford and Mr Gorringe.

A TYPICAL EXAMPLE of the splendid photographs of early this century, bearing no names, no date and no place. It seems to have been taken in the Crown meadow with Bryanston Cliff in the background.

Telegraphic Address : " Hammond, Blandford."
Telephone : No. 10.

Thomas Hammond

JOB and POST MASTER.
RIDING & LIVERY ESTABLISHMENT.

Temperance Hotel and Crown Hotel Mews,

BLANDFORD.

Superior Wedding Carriages Landaus, Brougham, Brakes,
Four in Hand   MODERATE CHARGES
HUNTERS, SADDLE and HARNESS HORSES always on hand
For Sale, Job or Hire   Improved Funeral Glass Car

Carriage Works. Station Approach.

IT IS CLEAR from this advertisement that Thomas Hammond had many irons in the fire early in the century.

MR F. CHRISTOPHER with J.L. Marsh's Brewery dray in the days when solid tyres were still in use.

THE PREMISES OF THE COATES FAMILY of Blandford at The Tabernacle with their carnival float ready to leave c. 1906. They were butchers, hay and corn dealers. The new Blandford Post Office went up on this site in 1935.

ACCIDENT IN WHITE CLIFF MILL STREET, Blandford in 1951 when a tank bumped into the house of Mr Champion. These cottages have since been demolished.

IN TIMES OF DROUGHT farmers and tradesmen had to collect water from the Stour via the old fording place on the Blandford St Mary side of the bridge.

THE BRIDGE, BLANDFORD.

ANOTHER VIEW OF THE BRIDGE looking west towards Blandford St Mary. Note the ornate gas lamp on the right.

ALFRED STEVENS, born at Blandford in 1817, sculptor, painter and industrial designer. He was a prizewinner at the Great Exhibition of 1851. Outstanding examples of his work include the seated lions outside the British Museum, the portrait of Mary Ann Collman in the National Portrait Gallery and the monument to the Duke of Wellington in St Paul's Cathedral. Dozens of his drawings and paintings hang in the Tate Gallery. He died in London in 1875 and is buried in Highgate Cemetery.

SAMUEL COWELL (1819–1864) the Famous music hall comedian. He performed before President Lincoln in the USA where he was very popular. However he took to drink and came to live with his friend Robert Eyers at The Crown Inn in Blandford. Cowell is buried at Blandford but his stone, which was known to have been in place in the 1970s, has mysteriously gone.

'SHEP' LOVELL, a well-known character in the Blandford area, seen here with twin Dorset Down lambs.

CONGESTION IN BLANDFORD'S SALISBURY STREET in 1906 at the time of the Charter Celebrations – Sharp's steam engine is in the procession and most of the town is in the street.

ROBERT SHARP'S FLOAT at Blandford Carnival in 1892. The children, from left to right, were: Lily Cross, Lynda Percy, Gladys Wareham, Percy Hare, May Hare, with Daisy Dyke at the back and Mr Parsons standing with the horse. They had first prize.

CHERRY'S (one of Blandford's old department stores) entered this float in the 1927 carnival.

THE BLANDFORD COAL MINE. George Best's float in around 1910. He is the tall man on the right and was a town councillor for many years.

J.L. MARSH & SONS' CARNIVAL FLOAT C. 1912, taken in the brewery yard with Mr Marsh on the right of the dray with the boys.

THREE INTREPID BLANDFORD LADIES on their motorcycles in the early 1920s. They were, left to right: Marjorie Conyers, Norah Westcott and Winifred Conyers.

BLANDFORD VOLUNTEER AMBULANCE CORPS 1912/13 with their horse-drawn ambulance behind them.

CORONATION STREET PARTY of 1953 somewhere on the Elizabeth Road estate area – with houses still under construction on the right.

A GROUP OUTSIDE THE CONGREGATIONAL CHURCH (UNITED REFORMED) in 1921 on the occasion of the dedication of the new organ. The Minister, the Revd Gomer Evans, is in the middle of the front row.

A MEETING OF THE PRIMITIVE METHODIST SYNOD at Blandford in 1932.

THE PRINCE OF WALES visits Blandford in 1923. He is the one in the bowler hat upon whom all eyes are directed.

A TEA PARTY GIVEN IN BRYANSTON PARK by the Mayor of Blandford, Edgar B. Smith, in 1897, the occasion being Queen Victoria's Diamond Jubilee.

A BATHING PARTY AT BLANDFORD in the late 1920s. Like boating, river bathing has long gone out of fashion.

THE STOUR does not freeze over to such an extent that it can be skated on very often. This picture was taken in 1963.

Milton Abbas School from the Garden, showing Gymnasium

THE REAR OF THE FORMER MILTON ABBAS GRAMMAR SCHOOL when at Blandford – the foreground is now the Gateway's car park.

BLANDFORD GYMNASTIC CLUB C. 1910. They met at the gymnasium behind Milton Abbas Grammar School. Among them are members of the Nesbitt, Hiscock, Bastable and Westcott families.

ROBERT DOWNES of the Blandford Blue-coat Charity School photographed in c. 1929. Each boy had a number from one to twelve to identify him and wore a gown, yellow or orange stockings and tam-o-shanter cap, belt and bib in the style of the boys of the present Christ's Hospital at Horsham. The school was founded in 1763 by William Wake, Archbishop of Canterbury (1715–1736) who was a native of Blandford Forum. The school closed in 1939.

BLUE-COAT BOYS AT PLAY c. 1930. Left to right: Victor Moors, Harry Whitlock, George Lowe, Robert Downes and William Charles Pike.

BLANDFORD INFANTS SCHOOL 1920. The teacher is Miss Butt. The little boy in the middle of the front row is Monty Cox — he still has the curls!

THOMAS HORLOCK BASTARD (who was in his one hundred and second year when he died in 1898) was founder of the former Milldown Endowed School in Blandford which became Blandford Secondary School and eventually Blandford Grammar School. He was Lord of the Manor of Charlton Marshall, the last Recorder of Blandford Forum and a Justice of the Peace.

THE SECONDARY SCHOOL in Damory Lane c. 1925. It became the Grammar School in 1928 and went 'comprehensive' before moving to Bryanston Deer Park to become the Upper School.

BLANDFORD GRAMMAR SCHOOL SPEECH DAY at Blandford Corn Exchange in November 1962.

BLANDFORD GRAMMAR SCHOOL PLAY in 1934/5. Back row: Alan Broadhurst, Sam Ridout (?), Donald Toms, Ralph White, Mr Watkins. Middle row: Henry Cox (?), Michael Venevitinoff, Fred Lewis. Front row: Joan Staff, Annie Upshall, Betty Elsworth.

BLANDFORD SECONDARY SCHOOL 1915/16, Form IV. Back row: Second left – Hubert Wyatt. Middle row: Second left – Maud Davis, Second right – Gladys Durdle.

BLANDFORD MEN, called up for duty in August 1914, assembled in West Street. Most are wearing bandoliers and spurs so were of the Dorset Yeomanry.

BLANDFORD MEN OF THE FIRST WORLD WAR from various services. It is probable that they had this taken at a time when they were on leave.

J.T. COUNTER. "VC."

JACK COUNTER, Blandford's only VC of the First World War, decorated for gallantry in France, 16 May 1918, when he carried vital messages under heavy fire after five of his comrades had been killed in the attempt.

THE COMRADES OF THE GREAT WAR (forerunners of the Royal British Legion) meet at Langton Manor House in July 1920.

SIR ROBERT BADEN-POWELL, Chief Scout, meets Blandford Councillors at a Scout Rally in 1929. He and Lady Baden-Powell were made Honorary Freemen of the borough on this occasion. The Mayor was W.J. Norman, Blandford's first Labour Councillor and Mayor.

LADY BADEN-POWELL with the Blandford Girl Guides in April 1929 at the Scout and Guide rally at Blandford.

SECTION THREE

Our Near Neighbours

BRYANSTON. Main lodge gates to driveway leading from Blandford Bridge to Bryanston House designed by Sir James Wyatt in 1778.

EDWARD BERKELEY PORTMAN (1799–1888) Liberal MP for Dorset and Marylebone. He married Lady Emma Lascelles, daughter of the Earl of Harewood, was created a Baron in 1837 and a Viscount in 1873.

THE OLD BRYANSTON MANOR HOUSE completed by Sir James Wyatt in 1778. It was demolished, except for the stables and some detached service buildings, in 1898 on completion of the new Bryanston House. The stone of the old house was used in the building of the new church of St Martin on the site. The chapel in the foreground is known as the Portman Chapel and is still standing.

WILLIAM HENRY BERKELEY, second Viscount Portman (1829/1919) a keen horseman who, like his father, lived to be 90. He was MP for Shaftesbury. He rebuilt the church at Durweston, was Master of the Portman Hunt and Chairman of Dorset County Council.

THE NEW MANOR HOUSE at Bryanston was completed in 1898 for the second Viscount Portman. It was built by Norman Shaw who was also the architect for New Scotland Yard. The last of the family to live there was Henry Berkeley Portman, the third Viscount, (1860–1923).

THE PORTMAN HUNT and estate grooms outside the service buildings of old Bryanston House in around 1880.

Lord Portman's Hounds.

THE PORTMAN HOUNDS with whom the second Viscount hunted until well into his 80s. The Hunt is still in existence.

A TEAM OF FARM WORKERS with their scythes near Blandford early in the century. Scythes continued in use for cutting round the borders of fields until the 1950s.

PORTMAN ESTATE WORKERS before the First World War building a haystack with the help of an elavator driven by an early petrol engine.

BLANDFORD ST MARY. Children learning rush-basket making in the Rectory yard. The Head Teacher here is Miss Mary E. Bint.

SCHOOLCHILDREN. c. 1895. The teachers standing are Miss Mabel Blanchard (left) and Miss M.E. Bint (right).

THE OLD ROAD from Dorchester passes Robert Sharp's seed shop and the New Inn and meets the road from Blandford Bridge into the village. The trees and greensward on the left are in Bryanston.

BRYANTS HOUSE is a survivor of the great Blandford Fire of 1731 which burned down many properties in this parish and Lower Bryanston.

HALL & WOODHOUSE'S DRAYS deliver to the New Inn (now the Stour Inn) c. 1914.

THE DOWN HOUSE was built in 1762 by Thomas Pitt, Lord of the Manor, largely rebuilt in the 1850s and burnt down in 1941. Only the stables now survive.

MEN OF THE BOTTLED BEER DEPARTMENT at Hall & Woodhouse's brewery c. 1920 – I date this by their caps.

'THE TUBBS' – the name given to the Hall & Woodhouse football team of the 1920s.

SHEEP KILLED BY LIGHTNING at William Hunt's farm at Thornicombe in June 1914. The shepherd's metal crook was given the blame!

OLIVER TURNER, known as 'Twisty' who made baskets and bee skeps at Thornicombe in 1941.

ST MARY'S MANOR HOUSE early in the century. The dormer windows are no longer there.

BLANDFORD ST MARY. A view into the village from Blandford Bridge where the parishes of Blandford Forum, Bryanston and Blandford St Mary meet.

THE GIRLS OF THE BLANDFORD ST MARY VILLAGE SCHOOL in 1906.

THE BOYS OF THE BLANDFORD ST MARY VILLAGE SCHOOL in 1906. A boy holds a slate of the type on which most of the written work was done.

LANGTON LONG. Old Langton Manor House was built by the great hunting squire J.J. Farquharson between 1827 and 1833. It was occupied as an HQ by the United States 2nd Division in the Second World War and was demolished in 1949.

LANGTON LONG. Activity behind cottages overlooking the Stour which were known as Londonderry – c. 1875.

THE GIRLS OF THE VILLAGE CHOIR at the parish church of All Saints, c. 1950.

SPECIAL SERVICES were held in the church in the 1930s for hikers and cyclists. The parson became known as the 'Hiker Parson.' The central figure on this occasion was the Rt. Revd Neville Lovett, Bishop of Salisbury.

THIS WAS ST LEONARD'S SCHOOL near the boundary with Blandford Forum. The site is now used for residential purposes and is known as Fisher's Close.

CHARLTON MARSHALL. A general view of the village approach from Blandford c. 1900.

THE OLD VILLAGE STOCKS now outside the parish church.

JOHN HORNER photographed c. 1880 with his straw carrier bags. He did a lot of shopping in Blandford for the old and infirm of the village.

A THATCHED COTTAGE on the Blandford side of the church. Some interesting carts and a man mending a punctured cycle tyre can be seen, c. 1905.

THE VILLAGE RAILWAY HALT was on the Somerset & Dorset Joint Railway. It was opened in 1928 with two simple platforms. It was closed with several others on this line in 1956.

SPETISBURY. Work in progress converting the Somerset & Dorset Line to double-line working between 1901 and 1905.

SPETISBURY STATION around 1925. Robert Cook the stationmaster has his sleeves rolled up. The station closed in 1956.

SPETISBURY STATION was opened in the 1890s. This is a very early train pulling in on a snowy day. Part of an early disc and bar signal can be seen on the left; they were discontinued in 1901.

THE VILLAGE STORES in the 1920s with the garage and filling station beyond. The shop is still serving the village.

THE SCENE IN SPETISBURY the day after the disastrous fire of 1905 which started in the village bakehouse.

St. Monica's Priory, Spettisbury

ST MONICA'S PRIORY, formerly Spetisbury House, was occupied by Augustinian Nuns followed by others of the Brigetine and Ursuline Orders. The Priory was sold in 1927 and parts of it remain in use for private residential purposes.

THE NUNS OF ST MONICA'S PRIORY ran a day and boarding school. This is a picture of some of the nuns and children in the Priory garden, c. 1910.

THE HALL & SLOPER VILLAGE SCHOOL founded by Dr Hall, Bishop of Bristol and Dr Sloper in 1728. Although now modernised and altered it is still in use.

DURWESTON. Durweston Mill on the River Stour early in the century – there has been a mill here since medieval times.

A GENERAL VIEW OF THE VILLAGE much as it looked in around 1912.

A MOTOR LORRY in trouble at Durweston Bridge in 1926. It was hauled out by Fred Sharp's steam engine from Blandford.

THE FORMER TURNPIKE COTTAGE near the bridge – Mr and Mrs Edwards are standing at the gate.

THE OPENING OF DURWESTON & STOURPAINE HALT in 1928. The two vicars and most of the inhabitants turned out. The Halt was closed in 1956.

POST OFFICE ROW opposite the church on the road to Bryanston.

HARRY RICKETTS (LEFT) and 'Sid' Tapper who were Portman Estate property maintenance men in the 1930s.

THE PARISH CHURCH OF ST NICHOLAS. There are several memorial stones in the churchyard to members of the Portman family.

KNIGHTON. A view of Knighton House on the Portman Estate. The second Viscount Portman lived here for 30 years following his marriage.

SHILLINGSTONE. The New Ox Inn on the Blandford to Sturminster Road as it was in late Victorian times. The Ansty brewery dray can be seen outside.

CHILDE OKEFORD. The Hollow with Crate Cottage and turning into Crate Lane on the left.

CHILDE OKEFORD. The village centre with the Baker Arms on the right of the picture and the butcher's shop adjoining. The Baker Arms are still licensed premises. The picture was taken in 1895.

TARRANT CRAWFORD. Crawford Bridge was built for the Nuns of Tarrant Abbey. It links that village with Spetisbury. The thatched cottages in the distance were destroyed by fire many years ago.

IWERNE COURTNEY (SHROTON). This village has two names. It was famous for its ancient fair which was one of the most popular in Dorset. This picture is of around 1910. It is immortalised in William Barnes' poem 'Shroden Feair'.

MILTON ABBAS. Joseph Arch, founder of the National Agricultural Labourers' Union was very active in the Milton Abbas/Blandford area. He spoke many times in Blandford in the 1870s. He is recorded as paying 4s. 10d. a night for his lodgings.

A FAMILY OF DORSET FARM WORKERS evicted from their cottage in 1874 for being members of Joseph Arch's Union.

TARRANT GUNVILLE. Rickmaking on the Farquharson estate early in the century.

A THREE-HORSE PLOUGH working on the heavy ground in the parish c. 1912.

A GENERAL VIEW OF TARRANT GUNVILLE. Here is buried Thomas Wedgewood, FRS (1771–1805) the pioneer photographer son of the famous potter, Josiah Wedgewood of Etruria.

A REAPER AT WORK in the parish, c. 1920.

TARRANT KEYNESTON. Horses being watered near the bridge in the 1920s.

THE TRUE LOVERS' KNOT public house on the Wimborne Road in around 1910. It is still licensed.

THE VILLAGE STORES C. 1910 with a baker's hand-cart outside and the True Lovers' Knot Inn in the background.

A CARRIERS CART (unidentified). These were very common in the district, over 30 being listed as travelling once or twice weekly to Blandford markets.

IWERNE MINSTER. The village scene of around 1906 with the parish church of St Mary in the distance.

PIMPERNE. Heavy horses at the village show in the 1930s. Left to right: Mr Motto Hall, carter for F. Sharp & Son, Langton. Jack Hansford, carter for C. Coats & Son, Pimperne. Charlie Bishop, carter for G. Mells & Son. Tarrant Gunville. Tom Priddle, carter for Major E.W.F. Castleman. Lou Hopkins, carter for A.H. Davis, Charlton Marshall. Sam Watts, carter for F. Sharp & Son, Langton.

CHARLES KINGSLEY (1819–75) was curate at Pimperne. He wrote *Westward Ho!* in 1855 and *The Water Babies* in 1863.

A VIEW OF THE MEDIEVAL VILLAGE CROSS and the church of St Peter which has a lovely Norman doorway. Most of the church was rebuilt in 1872/4 by Lord Portman.

REEVES VILLAGE STORES AND BAKERY in the early 1920s.

A GENERAL VIEW OF PIMPERNE. The long thatched building in the middle rear is now The Anvil public house. c. 1920.

TURNWORTH. A meal being prepared at a gypsy camp on the hills above the village, c. 1910.

BULBARROW. Dr Fielding attends a newly-born gypsy baby and its mother, with Sister Marlow in attendance.

HILTON. The Ansty Brewery of Hall & Woodhouse with delivery drays, c. 1908. The brewery was founded here in 1777.

THE ANSTY BREWERY COTTAGES at Hilton were occupied by employees. The cottages were destroyed by fire in 1985.

WALTER BROOMFIELD AND FAMILY in 1903. They were for many years at Cothayes Dairy, Ansty.

THE FORMER VILLAGE SCHOOL at Hilton built in 1863. It was closed a few years ago and has recently been converted for residential use.

MILTON ABBAS. The main village street before the removal of the chestnut trees between the houses in 1953.

THE VILLAGE SCHOOL built in 1853 and the Cottage Hospital built by Baron Hambro in 1873 to serve the parish and surrounding villages on his estate.

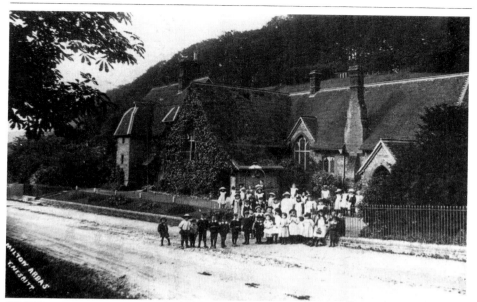

CHILDREN OUTSIDE THEIR SCHOOL in 1905. The school had two rooms and a master's house. There are 45 children in the picture only 10 of which were boys.

BEATERS photographed on the occasion of the visit of King Edward VII in 1909 for a few days' shooting as the guest of Baron Hambro.

THE FOOKES BROTHERS' BREWERY in 1880. Note the steam rising from the boiler at the back and the delivery dray.

THE BREWERY LORRY in 1930. Left to right: Ted Adams, Arthur Fookes, Henry Fookes.

STOURPAINE. The main Blandford to Shaftesbury Road, c. 1912. The White Horse Inn and garage are still there but the cottages on the left have all been demolished.

MANOR ROAD or Church Street, with the school of 1873 on the left, leading to Manor Farm and Holy Trinity Church, c. 1912.

A NICE MIXTURE of thatched and brick-banded and cob cottages c. 1912. Note the tradesman's van.

ANOTHER VILLAGE VIEW with the shop of Legg Bros., the butchers, on the left.

A STEAM ENGINE pulling a heavy plough by hawsers. The plough was pulled back to the other side of the field by another engine, c. 1914.

WINTERBORNE ANDERSON. A three-horse binder at work c. 1910.

WINTERBORNE HOUGHTON. A general view of the village, c. 1906, high up on the chalk. 'Cobblers Cottage' is on the right.

WINTERBORNE STICKLAND c. 1906, with The Rectory on the left and the former malthouse on the right.

NORTH STREET around 1905 with the Post Office on the left.

WINTERBORNE STICKLAND, c. 1912, looking towards the church of St Mary. The group on the bridge includes a young bandsman – most of the villages had a band at this time.

AN OVERTURNED STEAM ENGINE on Stickland Hill in 1904. Standing by are Mr G. Scovell and Mr Dunn.

THE ROAD TO MILTON ABBAS, c. 1910, with the village school of 1861 on the left.

THE TREE in the village centre where the roads meet, c. 1912.

WINTERBORNE KINGSTON. Duck Street in around 1905 with Bailey's Bakery and General Stores on the left.

ABBOTS COURT LANE with the former Bush Inn on the right before the motor car, c. 1912. The lane is now called East Street.

NORTH STREET – the Greyhound Inn sign can be seen at the top left of the street.

THE VILLAGE SCHOOL around 1910 – it is still there and a modern photograph would reveal little change.

THE WESLEYAN CHAPEL in Church Street was built in 1872.

WHITECHURCH ROAD, now called West Street, c. 1912. Cobblers Cottage and Arnold Cottage are on the right of the picture.

A VIEW OF THE VILLAGE from the south-west, c. 1912, with some activity in the field to the left of the road.

WINTERBORNE WHITECHURCH. The Post Office and Temperance Hotel. William Snook the postmaster is on the left, c. 1908.

THE VILLAGE as approached from Blandford, c. 1912.

OKEFORD FITZPAINE. A view of Lower Street taken around 1921.

THE OLD SCHOOL HOUSE is on the right of the picture, c. 1921. The new school was built in 1873. It can be seen in the far distance.

SECTION FOUR

The Military

CRIMEAN AND INDIAN WAR VETERANS at Blandford in 1907. The occasion was the fiftieth anniversary of the blowing up of the Cashmere Gate at Delhi.

A PROCESSION IN SALISBURY STREET, Blandford, in 1902 to honour the return of the Blandford Volunteers from the Boer War.

THE WALKING-OUT UNIFORM worn by members of the Blandford Troop of Dorset Imperial Yeomanry c. 1900.

A GENERAL VIEW of the Imperial Yeomanry's summer camp on Monkton Down, Blandford, c. 1912.

THE MOUNTED CAVALRY OF THE DORSET IMPERIAL YEOMANRY exercise at the summer camp at Blandford, c. 1912.

MEMBERS OF THE ROYAL ENGINEERS taking part in bridge-building training over the Stour at Blandford in 1916.

RUPERT BROOKE (1887–1915). The First World War poet whose works are still being printed. He came to Blandford Camp to join the Hood Batallion of the Royal Naval Division in 1914. Posted for service in Gallipoli in 1915, he died on board ship on 23 April and was buried on the Island of Skyros.

KING GEORGE V AND WINSTON CHURCHILL arrive at Blandford Station on 25 February 1915 to review the Royal Naval Division at Blandford Camp prior to its departure for Gallipoli.

A ROYAL NAVAL DIVISION AMBULANCE photographed at Blandford Camp in around 1916.

GERMAN PRISONERS OF WAR at Blandford Camp during the First World War. Most of them worked on the land for local farmers and probably thought themselves well out of the war.

A BLANDFORD CAMP DESPATCH RIDER of c. 1916. His mount seems to be a belt-driven Douglas with a huge fly-wheel.

AN OFFICER'S STAFF CAR pictured at Blandford Camp, c. 1917.

A WARTIME MOTORCYCLE COMBINATION used by the Royal Naval Division c. 1915/16. It had carbide lighting.

UNIFORMED STAFF of RAF Records at Blandford in 1919. Over 100 civilians were employed in addition to the enlisted staff.

THE RAF DOUBLE-DECKER used to convey civilian workers to and from the Camp prior to the construction of the branch railway line.

THE RAF RECORDS OFFICE FOOTBALL TEAM — December 1919.

REGULAR SOLDIERS waiting at Blandford station for the arrival of the first military conscripts to be posted to the camp in the summer of 1939.

THE CONSCRIPTS arrive at Blandford Station to be conveyed in trucks to the camp.

THE HUTTED CAMP AT BLANDFORD erected in the early years of the Second World War.

TARRANT RUSHTON AIRFIELD in 1944 with aircraft and gliders ready for the ill-fated battle for Arnhem. September 1944.

WAR CASUALTIES from France arrive at Tarrant Rushton airfield in 1944 for conveyance to the Blandford Camp hospital.

THE DUCHESS OF KENT, with the Commanding Officer of the United States 22nd General Hospital, Col. D.J. Fourrier, on the occasion of her tour of inspection in 1944.

UNITED STATES MILITARY POLICE at their headquarters in West Street, Blandford Forum, 1944.

UNITED STATES CONTROLLED POW COMPOUND at Blandford Camp for the accommodation of prisoners working on the camp.

THE MARRIAGE AT BLANDFORD PARISH CHURCH on 12 April 1944 of Capt. Quentin Roosevelt, a nephew of Franklin D. Roosevelt, to Frances Webb of the US Red Cross.

BLANDFORD GROUP ROYAL OBSERVER CORPS of the Second World War. Back, left to right: -?-, Hodge, Sprake, Denis, Westcott, -?-, -?-, Guy. Front: Gibbs, Moody, Wyatt, Carter, Winsor, -?-, Kail.

BLANDFORD HOME GUARD 1943/4 photographed outside their HQ at the Scout Hut leading off Eagle House Gardens.

THE ROADS AROUND THE CAMP were used for motorcycle racing between 1948 and 1960. Many famous riders, including Geoff Duke, competed here – he broke the lap record in 1950 at 91 mph!

PARADE OF THE DORSET REGIMENT in November 1955 in Blandford Market Place, on the occasion of the presentation of the Freedom of the Borough of Blandford.

THE MAYOR OF BLANDFORD, Alderman B.C. Hunt, presents the Freedom certificate to Major G.N. Wood, Colonel of the Dorset Regiment, on its being granted the Freedom.

THE ROYAL CORPS OF SIGNALS parade in Blandford Market Place on 13 October 1972 on the occasion of their being granted the Freedom of the Borough of Blandford.

REGIMENTAL BAND OF THE ROYAL CORPS OF SIGNALS at the October 1972 Freedom parade.

THE MAYOR OF BLANDFORD FORUM, Councillor A.N. Lane, and the Borough Council at the Royal Signals Freedom Ceremony in October 1972 awaiting the march past.

PRESENTATION to No.1 Training Batallion REME by the Mayor of Blandford, Councillor E.G. Riggs, in 1961 on the impending departure of the batallion from Blandford Camp.

ACKNOWLEDGEMENTS

For the earlier photographs included in my selection I have been fortunate in getting prints of pictures taken of the town and district by members of the Nesbitt family who carried on business as photographers in Blandford from around 1864 until the early 1920s. In addition, through the courtesy of Messrs. Hobbs & Sons Ltd., I have been able to borrow prints made by the late Mr Percival Hobbs, a former member of the firm, who was taking photographs for 25 years or more early in the century – he was more a keen amateur than a professional but his work was very good.

For more recent times I have been greatly helped by being able to draw on the collection of Sam and Betty Jardine who have been taking photographs here for the past 40 years or so and are still at it in their East Street studio.

The remainder represents a selection from the Blandford Museum's photographic collection which, thanks to the generosity of countless donors, I have been able to form in my capacity as Hon. Curator. I have needed a lot of help in putting names to faces and in this respect my thanks are here recorded to Charles Lavington, Monty and Wyn Cox, Fred Gould, Anne Hosford and my colleagues in the Blandford Museum Trust. Last, but not least, I should say a word of thanks to all those photographers of the past, whose prints I have, but who cannot be identified and to everyone who has contributed to the production of this book.